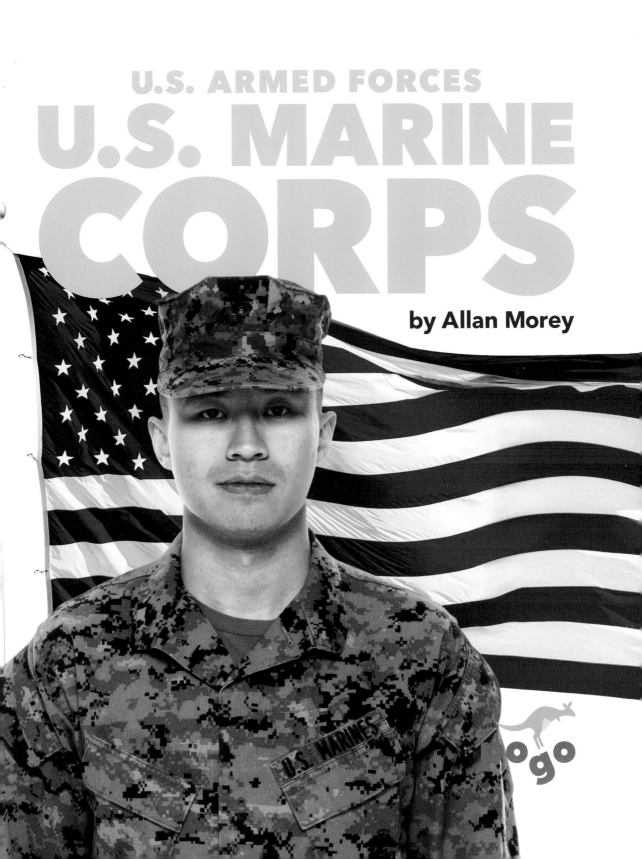

U.S. ARMED FORCES

U.S. MARINE CORPS

by Allan Morey

Ideas for Parents and Teachers

Pogo Books let children practice reading informational text while introducing them to nonfiction features such as headings, labels, sidebars, maps, and diagrams, as well as a table of contents, glossary, and index.

Carefully leveled text with a strong photo match offers early fluent readers the support they need to succeed.

Before Reading

- "Walk" through the book and point out the various nonfiction features. Ask the student what purpose each feature serves.
- Look at the glossary together. Read and discuss the words.

Read the Book

- Have the child read the book independently.
- Invite him or her to list questions that arise from reading.

After Reading

- Discuss the child's questions. Talk about how he or she might find answers to those questions.
- Prompt the child to think more. Ask: Before reading this book, did you know what types of jobs U.S. Marines perform? What more would you like to learn about the U.S. Marines?

Pogo Books are published by Jump!
5357 Penn Avenue South
Minneapolis, MN 55419
www.jumplibrary.com

Library of Congress Cataloging-in-Publication Data

Names: Morey, Allan, author.
Title: U.S. Marine Corps / by Allan Morey.
Description: Minneapolis, MN: Jump!, [2021]
Series: U.S. Armed Forces
Audience: Ages 7-10 | Audience: Grades 2-3
Identifiers: LCCN 2019049857 (print)
LCCN 2019049858 (ebook)
ISBN 9781645274254 (hardcover)
ISBN 9781645274261 (ebook)
Subjects: LCSH: United States.
Marine Corps—Juvenile literature.
Classification: LCC VE23 .M63 2021 (print)
LCC VE23 (ebook) | DDC 359.9/60973—dc23
LC record available at https://lccn.loc.gov/2019049857
LC ebook record available at https://lccn.loc.gov/2019049858

Editor: Susanne Bushman
Designer: Molly Ballanger

Content Consultant: Staff Sergeant Isaac Reich, U.S. Marine Corps

Staff Sergeant Isaac Reich served in the U.S. Marine Corps for eight years as an Aviation Mechanic, inspecting and servicing F-18, C-130, and F-35 aircraft. He continued his education by attending advanced composite repair school and non-destructive inspection school. He served in Japan in 2015.

Photo Credits: Yeongsik Im/Shutterstock, cover; 4x6/iStock, 1 (foreground); turtix/Shutterstock, 1 (background); U.S. Marine Corps, 3, 4, 6-7, 10, 11, 12-13, 14-15, 16-17, 18, 20-21, 23; Lance Cpl. Kenny Nunez Bigay/U.S. Marine Corps, 5; Cpl. Reece Lodder/U.S. Marine Corps, 8-9; Greg Mathieson/Getty, 19.

Printed in the United States of America at Corporate Graphics in North Mankato, Minnesota.

TABLE OF CONTENTS

FIRST TO ACTION

An **amphibious** vehicle lands on a beach. Marines charge out. They are ready for action!

amphibious
vehicle

Marines are trained to act fast. They are always ready for **combat** and are often the first in action. Many of their **missions** are overseas.

The Marine Corps is part of the U.S. Navy. Its members are called Marines. They help protect the United States and its **allies**. How? They protect at sea, on land, and in the air.

DID YOU KNOW?

The Marine Corps is a **branch** of the U.S. military. Others include:
- U.S. Air Force
- U.S. Army
- U.S. Coast Guard
- U.S. Navy

The National Guard is like a branch. But the states run it. The branches are run by the **federal government**.

U.S. Air Force
transport airplane

Marines work with other military branches, too. U.S. Air Force planes **transport** Marines. U.S. Navy ships do, too. All of the branches protect the United States.

CHAPTER 2

MARINE CORPS JOBS

Marine **recruits** go to boot camp. There, they learn the skills they'll need. This includes physical training. They have to complete an obstacle course.

Recruits run. They do sit-ups and pull-ups. They must be strong swimmers. Why? Marines are often at sea.

Next, they go to the School of **Infantry**. They learn how to use special weapons. They get combat training. Some learn to drive special vehicles. They may join a combat **unit**.

TAKE A LOOK!

Marines have **ranks**. They start as Privates. Then they move up! They get **insignia**. We often see them on their **dress blues**.

INSIGNIA

 Sergeant Major of the Marine Corps

 Sergeant Major

 Master Gunnery Sergeant

 First Sergeant

 Master Sergeant

 Gunnery Sergeant

 Staff Sergeant

 Sergeant

 Corporal

 Lance Corporal

 Private First Class

Some Marines train for jobs.
Like what? They can study
to be electricians.

Marines with college
degrees can become
officers. Then they go to
Officer Candidate School.
Why? They learn how
to lead others.

Raiders are a **special force**. They go on secret missions. Like what? They sneak into enemy lands. They attack the enemy or rescue people. They might work with other special forces, too.

WHAT DO YOU THINK?

The **motto** of the Marines is "Semper Fidelis." It means "always faithful." Marines are faithful to their country and each other. What does this mean to you?

Raider

CHAPTER 3
MANY MISSIONS

Marines go on many missions. During war, they often fight in cities.

A special unit fights **terrorists**. It helps when terrorists attack the United States. It also helps other countries fight. Its members will help anywhere in the world.

In 2017, a hurricane hit Texas. Many areas flooded. Marines helped. They rescued people. They brought others food. How? They used amphibious vehicles.

U.S. Marines protect and serve around the world. Would you like to be a Marine?

DID YOU KNOW?

The U.S. president directs all military branches. He or she decides where to send them. We call the president the Commander in Chief.

QUICK FACTS & TOOLS

TIMELINE

1775
The Continental Marines is formed during the Revolutionary War (1775–1783).

1942
The Marine Corps Raiders are established during World War II (1939–1945).

1945
The U.S. Marine Corps captures the island of Iwo Jima from Japanese forces.

1987
The Marine Fleet Anti-Terrorism Security Team is formed.

2017
Marines perform rescue missions in Texas after Hurricane Harvey.

U.S. MARINE CORPS MISSION

The mission of the U.S. Marine Corps is to win the nation's battles swiftly and aggressively in times of crisis. They fight on land, sea, and air, as well as provide forces and detachments to naval ships and ground operations.

U.S. MARINE CORPS ACTIVE DUTY MEMBERS:

around 184,000 (as of 2019)
Active duty members serve full-time.

U.S. MARINE CORPS RESERVE MEMBERS:

around 104,000 (as of 2019)
Reserve members train and serve part-time.

GLOSSARY

allies: Countries that are on the same side during wars or military actions.

amphibious: Having to do with both land and water.

branch: One of the groups of the U.S. military, including the U.S. Air Force, U.S. Army, U.S. Coast Guard, U.S. Marine Corps, and U.S. Navy.

combat: Fighting.

dress blues: The formal uniforms Marines wear to special events.

federal government: The central government of the United States.

infantry: The foot soldiers of an army.

insignia: Symbols that show the ranks of people in the military.

missions: Tasks or jobs.

motto: A short sentence or phrase that states a belief or is used as a rule for behavior.

ranks: Positions in the military.

recruits: New members of a military force.

special force: A specialized military group that is trained to do particular tasks.

terrorists: People who use violence and threats in order to frighten people, obtain power, or force governments to do things.

transport: To carry from place to place.

unit: A group of Marines.

INDEX

TO LEARN MORE

Finding more information is as easy as 1, 2, 3.

① Go to www.factsurfer.com

② Enter "U.S.MarineCorps" into the search box.

③ Click the "Surf" button to see a list of websites.

FACT SURFER